How to Be an Amazon Legend and Fire Your Banker!

By Danny Stock & Mark Willis
©2018

Dedications

I dedicate this book to all the people who work every day and wonder, "Is this all? Is this it? Is this what I'm to do the rest of my life?" Then they look to the horizon and realize there may be far more.

I also want to dedicate this book to my wife and family who support me all along the way and enable me to realize my dreams. ~ Danny Stock

I dedicate this book to the entrepreneur. The one who has the courage to see things differently, and as a result has the bravery to change the world.

I also dedicate this book to my wife and daughter who bring joy to my life and thankfulness to my heart. ~ Mark Willis

Danny Stock & Mark Willis

Table of Contents

Dedications   iii

Special Note About the Writing
     of This Book   7

1 - Americans Are in Trouble   9

2 - Entrepreneurs are the Risk Takers
     in Our Economy…   15

3 - …but Bankers are Ready to Swoop
     in and Take Entrepreneur Profits   19

4 - Your Online Business on Amazon
     Gives You More Control Over
     Your Business and Life…   29

5 - …and Bank On Yourself® Gives
    You More Control Over
    Your Finances   39

6 - Build a Permanent Line of Credit
    for Your Amazon Business   51

7 - Use the Policy Loan Feature for
    Inventory (Repay on Your Terms)   57

8 - Bank On Yourself is a Warehouse of
    Wealth for Your Amazon Profits!   67

9 - Use Bank On Yourself to Pay
    off Your Debts to Amazon Lending
    and to Other Creditors   75

Conclusion   81

Disclaimers   89

Special Note About the Writing of This Book

The authors, Danny Stock and Mark Willis offer complementary viewpoints on how you can become an Amazon Legend, but each provides his own unique voice and background.

Danny and Mark wrote their own sections instead of co-mingling their writing. This gives you, the reader, helpful insight into their personalities and how each can help in their own way.

To serve you best, each author's writing has been prefaced by the author's name with a heading that lets you know whose section you're about to read.

Therefore, you'll find each author's writing section begins with either *Danny Writes* or *Mark Writes*.

Danny Stock & Mark Willis

1
-
Americans Are in Trouble

Mark Writes

Americans are in trouble.

What once was Manifest Destiny, is now primarily festering debt, what once was the American Dream, has become a mortgage drain, and where once we had solid savings ready to weather a decade-long depression, now the little we can avoid spending goes straight into speculation.

And yet, out of this vortex of trouble we may yet find a huge opportunity for those that look for it.

What Happened?

First, let's figure out what happened.

This report starts as a whodunit: you'll find here an autopsy of the American entrepreneur and the financial situation of the average American today. We need to know what happened, and then we can offer a strategy that is already helping thousands of Americans and Canadians who would like to recapture the spirit of freedom that founded this land.

Paul Poirot, author of a little known, out-of-print book titled, *The Pension Idea* is quoted as saying:

> *What Security is to be found in the world?*
>
> *The answer lies in the minds and in the hands of individuals, each of whom can enjoy as much security as he is willing to earn and is free to save.*

Whatever security has been lost to individuals in the United States can be recovered only through the taking back of the liberty in which persons have given up and in the illusion that personal responsibility can be shifted to someone else.

The tasks requires that every man/woman think for himself/herself and understand how the source of one's own security is to be found within himself/herself.

If we zoom way out and look back over the last century, we can see a slow erosion of personal freedom being taken away from the individual and given over (mostly willingly) to others. Whether a corporation, or our government, and to our banker, or our broker, we have seen the slow shift of our ability to find security in our freedom and have chosen slavery instead.

Since 1940, Americans have gone from saving 27% to saving 2.6% as of 2018. Simultaneously, according to the US Department of Commerce Bureau of Economic Analysis, we have moved from servicing debt at 11% to an average of 35.9%.

Let that sink in.

A Nation of Debtors

Let that sink in.

We have moved from being a nation of savers, to being a nation of debtors. If time is money, then we are, on average, slaves to a bank for more than a third of our lives. If you take taxes into consideration (with all the "security" we have asked of Uncle Sam), we can only hope to be free for a few hours a day. Most of us spend those moments of freedom being preached to by commercials that demand we surrender still more freedom and security (*Eat this! You're fat! Buy this and feel complete!*).

The vortex of debt, and the surge of more and more luxuries in our life has drained our ability to save a meager 2.6% of our income.

Will that be enough to cover the flat tires, the leaking roofs, the kids' college funds, our medical emergencies, and our eventual retirement? No way!

When I sit down with folks, one subtle but pervasive belief I hear in the subtext of our conversations around savings goes something like this:

> *"Well, I'm trapped by my debts and my expensive lifestyle. Therefore, I will just have to save less. But to make up for it, I'll put what little savings I can into riskier and riskier assets, and hope and pray to get a higher rate of return."*

These aren't just the folks in my office; you can hear this whisper across the last few decades, as we've seen the drop in savings, the rise of the credit card, and the emergence of the average American putting their retirement into Wall Street.

We've gone from savers to "investors."

Saving isn't sexy - investing is! Thus, was born the likes of the 401(k), the IRA, day trading, mutual funds, ETFs, and now crypto-speculation.

But for all our striving and financial sophistication, are we any more secure?

How do we, like Paul Poirot suggests, find the source of security in ourselves?

2
-
Entrepreneurs are the Risk Takers in Our Economy...

Mark Writes

One of the more promising developments in the last decade has been the rise of the entrepreneur. She has become the symbol of freedom and has even seen a resurgence from the ashes of the Great Recession of 2008.

According to the Global Entrepreneurship and Development Index, the United States is the top country in the world for developing entrepreneurs (out of 138 countries) and according to the Kauffman Foundation, a whopping 6.02% of Americans work on their own business as their primary job!

The Way Out

We instinctively know as a nation that entrepreneurship is a way out of the problems of debt.

We revere the entrepreneur and the self-made billionaire through hit TV shows like *Shark Tank*. The entrepreneur gives back some of the control that as a nation we believe we have lost in the last half-century.

We revere them as heroes who risk it all, and who believe in themselves rather than outsourcing their responsibility to others, taking it upon themselves to build security and financial freedom. They are the very embodiment of Paul Poirot's quote in chapter one about finding the source of security in ourselves.

Entrepreneurs

As a *CERTIFIED FINANCIAL PLANNER*™ I'm trained to look at entrepreneurs in a special way.

I see them as risk takers but only taking on the necessary risks needed to improve their odds at success. The reality is that most entrepreneurs I meet are fairly conservative with the rest of their portfolio.

For example, they often want a large pool of contingency capital both for emergencies and opportunities. That means *COLD, HARD CASH* on hand ready to go for any reason. They often liquidate their 401(k) or IRA in order to help grow their businesses, drain their savings, and even call on the angel investors of family and friends to chip in.

The Slow Rise of New Businesses

While we can certainly sing the praises of the rise of the entrepreneur, we have noticed a distinct lack of new businesses starting up since the financial crisis.

Why?

We believe it is because banks have had a stranglehold on Americans' ability to take control of their finances and take the leap in starting a business.

Let's learn more in the next chapter.

3

-

...but Bankers are Ready to Swoop in and Take Entrepreneur Profits

Mark Writes

While I'm certainly soft for the entrepreneurial journey (being a small business owner myself), I often find that entrepreneurs let their children and family suffer. They can fail to prepare for their own retirement in hopes of seeing their business dreams come true. They've put all their chips on the table.

Whereas most financial planners will tell you to "diversify," most entrepreneurs have put all their money into their business –it's a "one asset portfolio."

The Banker

Unfortunately, the foil of unsuccessful entrepreneurs is the banker.

Yes, banks and high interest debt have even found their way into the business models of entrepreneurs, the last freedom icons and demigods of our society.

Of all businesses that fail, according to Business Insider[1], 82% of them attribute their failure to cash flow problems and 21% of all entrepreneurs[2] have resorted to using credit cards to operate their business.

Many have drained their savings, mortgaged the house, and added more on personal loans, bank loans, and credit cards.

Still more businesses die before they're even given a chance to live. Many would-be entrepreneurs are still paying off a $1.3 trillion-dollar mountain of student loan

---

[1] http://www.businessinsider.com/why-small-businesses-fail-infographic-2017-8

[2] https://www.hiscox.com/blog/hiscox-dna-american-entre-preneur-2015

debt, which now exceeds credit card debt in this country.[3]

With even seniors getting social security checks garnished to pay back student loans, how can we expect folks to take a risk leaving their wage-based job to start the next Apple or Tesla?

We contend that banks are the problem… and privatized banking is the solution.

But we're getting ahead of ourselves.

A Closer Look at the Banking Process

Banking is the most profitable business in the history of man.

Think about that statement for a moment.

When you walk into a bank and deposit $1,000 into your savings account, what does the bank do with it? Does the bank

---

[3] https://www.forbes.com/sites/zackfriedman/2017/02/21/student-loan-debt-statistics-2017/

keep it all in their vault? Of course not! The bank loans it to the guy behind you in line at the bank requesting a loan.

How much of that $1,000 is the bank required to keep on their books? Ten percent (10%) is the official number,[4] but in 2008, we found out that many banks only had 2% on reserve.

So, you give the bank $1,000, and the bank pays you .01% for the privilege of using your money for their profits. Then the bank loans $900 to Bob behind you in line for 10%.

(That's a 100,000% rate of return!)

But Bob doesn't just walk out with $900 in cash. What *does* he do?

He deposits it into *his* bank account of course!

---

[4] https://www.newyorkfed.org/research/epr/02v08n1/0205benn/0205benn.html

So, the bank gets to do this incredible accounting (magic) trick of creating money over and over again!

So, Bob has now deposited $900 from his bank loan, and the bank must keep $90 on the books, and loan out another $810 to Jill at 10% interest… it's a runaway financial flywheel for the banks!

So far, the initial deposit of $1,000 caused the creation of another $1,710 (Bob's $900 + Jill's $810).

Real Money Dwindles

This process continues until all the "real money" has been dwindled down. Of course, the customers of the bank don't even realize this is happening to their money, until they all do a "run on the bank" during a financial panic and find that there is no money at the bank!

And yet, the bank created insane amounts of wealth for its owners out of thin air. This process is known as "fractional reserve banking," and this is the primary reason why you see banks listed as the major institutions in every town and city center, naming sport stadiums, and in the pockets and ears of every politician.

The Entrepreneur Takes the Risks

The truth is, banks are reaping all the profits, and have handed all the risks to the entrepreneur.

Think about it… how much risk did the bank take on you when you took out that bank loan to start or grow your business? None! They've got all your equipment, or inventory, as collateral to repossess if you can't pay them back. Or they'll sue you and get it all back in court.

And they'll charge interest.

Does the bank care if you had a bad month selling inventory? Or had a family or health crisis that took you away from the business for a few weeks or months? No, and in return, they'll wreck your credit, call you day and night, and send you threatening letters demanding payment. They'll squeeze you till you have repaid every penny.

Not much has changed since King Solomon wrote the proverb, "The borrower is *slave* to the lender." (Proverbs 22:7) (emphasis added)

You are already in the banking business. We all are. It's like Neo in *The Matrix* - when he woke up to realize the entire human population was plugged into the machine, he couldn't un-see it. Not only did he immediately break free from his constraints, but he became devoted to the cause of freeing the world from this enslavement by the machines. If you are loaded up with bank debt, credit cards, lines of credit, student loans and mortgages, you are part of the banking matrix.

Everyone is Affected

If you are feeling slightly smug and saying to yourself, "Well that is a real problem for others, but I pay cash for *everything*, this doesn't affect *me*," let me be the first to inform you, unfortunately, you are still wrapped up in the banking operations cartel.

First, as a saver you are participating with banks in the nightmare of "fractional reserve banking" in that every dollar you keep on deposit at the bank is contributing to the inflation of the money supply and you pay for it in the pathetically small interest rates paid on your savings.

You are punished as a saver.

Second, and this is very important, *you finance everything you buy.* Think about it; when you save up and pay cash for things, you lose all the interest you could have earned on that money had you not spent the money and left it invested instead.

Either you pay interest to banks, or you pass up unearned interest by spending money you'll never see grow for you again.

What Can We Do?

So where is that red pill Neo is famous for choosing? How do we unplug ourselves from the banking system?

In one way, we can't. As entrepreneurs, we must participate in the world economy. Unless you plan to start trading pinecones instead of greenbacks, we will have to find a way to involve ourselves in the system.

So why not use that system to *your* advantage? If banking is your problem today, let's make it part of your solution.

Like a judo fighter, who uses the weight and strength of his opponent to his advantage, what if you could become the banker to yourself and play their game of letting your money do more than one thing at once?

What if you could loan yourself the cash you need for your business to survive and thrive?

What if you could set your own repayment terms? What if you could remove the fees and painstaking paperwork involved in traditional bank loans? What if you could not only avoid the pain of traditional bank financing, but instead use the concept of banking to your advantage?

That's what the rest of this report is all about.

4
-
Your Online Business on Amazon Gives You More Control Over Your Business and Life...

Danny Writes

Let me tell you about my 8-year long fight with life and money.

It was September 19, 2006 and I was on Ft. Bragg in the Army going through an extremely grueling and physically challenging training for my specialization. At that time, I had no idea that day would forever change my life.

On that day, Amazon issued a press release that they would be opening a new part of their business development called *Fulfilled by Amazon*, also known as *FBA*. Amazon was giving small businesses the opportunity to tap into their vast and proven infrastructure. Amazon was giving individuals such as myself a network that took years and millions of dollars to build, thus creating many future million-aires and new businesses based around this FBA concept.

Their action caught retailers off guard and with one swift move, Amazon left the competition behind and set a new standard in customer service and shipping speeds for online shoppers.

Amazon and Me

I was aware of Amazon, but I would never have thought I would be building a full-time income from Amazon while working part time.

But, I would not figure this all out until eight years later… so back to my story.

Challenges

The only thing on my mind back then was surviving the physical challenges pre-sented to me every day. I thought only about making it to the next meal so that I could have at least a short reprieve from our physical and mental conditioning. Not to mention, I had a constant insatiable appetite for food since our bodies burned more calories than we could possibly consume on any given day.

I remember in December of 2006 that we were near the end of our training and sitting in a classroom receiving instruction on tactics. During that class, a Lieutenant Colonel walked in and wanted to talk to a few of us. He started to call off about half a dozen names which included myself and my best friend Jeff who I had joined the service with. As we followed the Lt. Colonel outside, I just had this sinking feeling; in what seemed like a time period of only a few seconds, he let us know that we were going to be deployed to Iraq shortly after our training completed.

Even though I was aware of the possibility of being deployed, I recall feeling alone and lost. I felt that my world was completely turned upside down. The butterflies in my stomach were so intense as we headed back in. I felt so heavy as we walked back in to our class.

All I recall about the rest of my time there was having a nagging feeling and fear of the unknown. To this day, I have trouble remembering anything that happened after that except our graduation and going home.

Later

Let us fast forward to May 3rd, 2010. This marked a day of joy and uncertainty in my life. Our daughter Clara was born 3 months premature weighing in at only 1 pounds, 9 ounces. Because of some complications that my wife Mia experienced, I was completely and utterly helpless during the next 97 days as Clara fought for survival in the NICU. I was working full time in our family contracting business and Mia was on summer break from her teaching job, so she was able to be up there every day with Clara because of the wonderful Ronald McDonald House charities.

I had to stay back and continue to earn some income in order to keep everything paid for and visited the weekends.

Looking back now, the summer of 2010 was a hectic one as I worked long hours at work and came home and made strides in fixing up our house for the arrival of Mia and Clara. Finally, later that summer, Mia and Clara were able to come home. It was a joyous day!

The Joy was Turned into a Dark Cloud

Unfortunately, that was all short lived. Mia received notice from the school she worked at that they were going to let her go because they assumed she was not coming back to work due to Clara and her condition. I remember thinking, "You've gotta be kidding me!"

So, this began a dark period for us financially and we ran up credit card debts, refinanced our house, sold our car as well as many other possessions just to make ends meet.

It was an exhausting time in our lives. I felt myself in a constant pursuit for answers to our financial struggles. In this pursuit for answers, I spent hundreds if not a thousand hours over the course of a year digging deep and looking for answers and the secrets of financial success on the internet. I had investigated and researched dozens and dozens of financial instruments and strategies to make money online and doing that from home.

Finally, one evening, I stumbled across a website talking about couponing and finding good deals at stores and selling them on Amazon.com.

From that moment on my life forever changed!

Online Selling

When I learned the power of selling online and how super simple and zero risk it was (yes, it is zero risk with the strategies I implement), I was completely in love with the whole idea of being able to sell to anyone in world and potentially work from home full time.

When I started this online selling adventure, I was working as a contractor with the family business and Mia had found a part-time teaching job at a local college. Money was still extremely tight, and we were still completely broke. I decided to go an additional $800 in debt and start buying some inventory to sell on Amazon.

In a few short months, we sold 40 thousand dollars of merchandise and we were bringing in more money than our two jobs combined! It took me another two years before I decided to quit the contracting business and my wife quit her job as well to stay home with our only daughter at the time.

Business Boomed

Over the next year, our business just completely skyrocketed!

In 2015, we found out that we were having another girl and as you might guess, she ended up being born early just like her older sister Clara was. Luckily, Charlotte was only born a month early and had a much shorter and less scary stay at the NICU.

By this time, we were able to pay for any medical costs with cash that were not covered under our policy. This gave me a sense of pride because I was able to provide for my family in that way.

About this same time, we had managed to pay off all of our personal debt and finally reached equilibrium with our finances and started saving money. 2015 is a special year for me as you can see, and it ended our eight-year period of financial and personal struggles.

As of this writing, I have sold millions of dollars of physical and non-physical products online at Amazon.com and my own website.

The beautiful part about this is that I work from home where my wife, Mia, is a stay-at-home Mom with our two daughters and they are homeschooled. We enjoy countless hours together in our home living our dream.

None of this could be possible without some hard work and leveraging the ease of selling on Amazon and doing all of my work online. We also have the luxury to take vacations when we want, since our whole business and schooling is portable.

I wish for everyone to be able to enjoy the same freedoms I have both financially and physically. If you care to follow me on my journey you can stay in touch with me at amzlegends.com.

Danny Stock & Mark Willis

5
-
...and Bank On Yourself® Gives You More Control Over Your Finances

Danny Writes

We moved from the 95% to the 5%.

So, what does it mean to move from the 95% to the 5%? Well, if you have read any of the *Rich Dad, Poor Dad* books by Robert Kiyosaki, then you know what I am talking about. In those, he provides a graph that shows on one side people who are "E" employed or "S" self-employed. On the other side of the graph, he shows "I" Investor and "B" business owner.

Below the graph he mentions some statistics that show the employed and self-employed make up 95% of the populace, but only earn 5% of the wealth. It's the investors and business owners who make up 5% of the populace and earn 95% of the wealth!

This is an astonishing statistic and it really made me realize that I wanted to be on the business owner and investor side of the equation. In my Amazon business, I had already made the transition from self-employed to the business owner by building a system and outsourcing it. I now wanted to figure out the investment piece. What I had not realized is that it was already sitting right in front of me!

A Legacy

Back when my wife and I were in financial troubles, I spent many hours studying ways to invest and do so wisely.

I tried a multitude of investment strategies but none of them provided any long-term, dependable growth. I knew I wanted to have at least one thing in my life that I could bank on when I retired and the stock market and all the traditional investments I investigated seemed highly risky.

Wondering if I was going to face a financial downturn right before I "retired" was not something I wanted to think about. It was important to me that I was able to leave behind a legacy for my family.

"Bank On Yourself"

I had heard the phrase "bank on yourself" many times before, and that little voice inside me kept telling me to do something with it in a big way. I found Mark through the Bank On Yourself® website and I made the call.

We had a smaller insurance policy at the time, but our business had grown to the point that we were able to put aside more savings. When I talked to Mark on the phone, we talked about my family, what I envisioned with this new policy, and how my financial position and needs had changed.

The one key thing that I had never really considered was how flexible the Bank On Yourself type policy was and what a perfect fit it provided for my current business model of buying and selling things on Amazon and other websites.

Today

Fast forward to today. We have built a very nice nest egg within the cash value of our policy and if something were to happen to me, my wife Mia, a stay-at-home Mom, would not experience financial trouble and she could continue to stay at home and care for our children. What a relief that is to me knowing that every day when I wake up, my family is protected and provided for financially.

Mark Writes

We've made some audacious claims so far in this book, and we're not done yet.

What if I told you that you could become your own source of financing, and fire your banker? What if I told you that you already have that within your power, that you don't have to wait for Congress to pass some resolution or form some new finance regulatory committee?

What Exactly Is the Bank On Yourself Concept?

Banking happens; it is a function of our lives. The question is, do you control the banking function in your life, or have you given that control away to someone else?

We've learned in the previous chapters that banking is a source of major anxiety and trouble for most of us. But it doesn't have to be this way. What if you could "Bank On Yourself"?

Let's examine the Bank On Yourself concept and learn how it helps you in your journey to become financially free. Bank On Yourself is the concept of becoming your own source of financing, building for yourself a source of capital by which you could borrow, and paying the capital back on your terms.

Can you imagine your life and your business if you just had that large pool of contingency capital ready to deploy when opportunities (or emergencies) came along?

It sounds like a nice concept, but how do we do it?

To "Bank On Yourself," you need a tool – and not many of us have the power of Congress or the might of a mega-bank to create exotic financial vehicles that allow the small business to bring their financing needs back in-house. This tool would need to be safe, predictable, and liquid. It would need minimal to zero red-tape to get your cash and provide ample flexibility in funding. It would need to avoid hefty taxes, fees, and commissions to keep it lean and effective for the business owner's needs. The interest paid on loans to your own financing strategy would somehow need to benefit you - rather than line the pockets of another banker. Finally, if we could keep all this private and outside of the reach of creditors (in the event of business difficulty or bank-ruptcy), that would make sure this plan worked even if the business failed to make it.

So, does a tool like this actually exist (and is it legal)? The answer is yes and yes!

After searching for tools that would solve all these problems and more, I discovered that, of all things, a little-known variation of a 160-year old financial product, divi-dend paying whole life insurance, mod-ernized for maximum cash value accumu-lation can do all this.

How is that?

Two Kinds of Life Insurance

There are two kinds of life insurance (speaking broadly of course) - the kind you rent, and the kind you own.

Term insurance is what most of us are taught about. Term insurance lets you pay a small premium to borrow a death bene-fit. It's like renting! Term life gets more expensive each birthday you have (the landlord is raising the rate on you!), and there is no "equity" in your term insurance policy, just like renting an apartment.

In contrast, your dividend-paying whole life insurance policy is like owning a home. You have the death benefit just the same, but you also have "equity" or cash value in your policy. Whole life builds and grows on a guaranteed schedule every single year, no matter what is happening in the markets.

On top of those guarantees, you have the potential to earn dividends (profits) from the insurance company.

It needs to be stated that dividends are not guaranteed, but there are companies that have paid them every year consecutively for over 100 years, including the years throughout the Great Depression! This is only possible because you are in essence, an owner in the life insurance company (mutual) and it's not publicly traded on Wall Street.

Furthermore, this particular type of whole life is liquid and available to you for whatever reason. Its cash value is made ready for you in the event of a business need, a vacation, a home repair, a medical event, or anything else your heart desires.

You can take a withdrawal or borrow from the cash value.

When you use the loan feature on certain policies (when designed correctly), your cash value will continue to give you the same guaranteed annual cash value increase and same dividend you would have received had you not borrowed from it. What? That can be confusing, so let's say that again: your money keeps growing, even on the capital you borrow, as if you never touched a dime of it.

That's only when you have a feature known as a "non-direct recognition life insurance policy loan provision" – that's a mouthful, but the good news is that your money is given the opportunity to do what bank money does - work more than one thing at once!

An Example to Clarify

Imagine if you had a $100,000 in a normal, boring savings account. Let's say in generosity that it was earning 5% a year. (At the time of this writing, I know of *no* savings account doing this - if you find any, let me know!)

This would mean that if you left your $100,000 in savings, you'd earn $5,000 for the privilege of not touching your cash. Of course, the bank could be loaning this out at 10% interest, keeping only a fraction on their books and making tremendous profits. If you were to choose to withdraw $30,000 to buy a car, you'd only earn interest on the remaining $70,000 ($3,500).

But what about these Bank On Yourself policies? If one is designed with this non-direct feature in mind, you could borrow $30,000 from the policy, but still receive the same growth and dividends on the full $100,000.

This is how you take the banking function and bring it in house.

The cash value in the policy is available now as mentioned, but it is also building and growing every single year, toward your retirement. It becomes another stream of income in your golden years.

If the policy is structured correctly, the money in the policy can be accessed tax-free through a combination of withdrawals and non-recourse loans (these are loans you don't have to repay) and are simply forgiven by reducing your death benefit when you pass away.

Going Forward

The vast majority of insurance companies out there do not offer all these features, but what I found as I discovered and learned more about this is that the wealthiest in the nation have this same tool in their portfolio, and they use it regularly to make major purchases.

A client of mine recently attended a financial and business planning workshop with a well-known business owner and former presidential candidate worth over $500 million dollars. He described in detail his *seventeen* life insurance policies that he has in his portfolio, and how each one of his family is a part of the support system for his family.

Do you see how this would add some considerable flexibility, and a competitive edge to your life, your family, and your business?

The good news is this is not some exotic financial instrument only available to the ultra-high net worth individuals or major multinational corporations. It doesn't require some major act of Congress. It's already available for you, me, and all of us right now.

What follows is just a few ways you could use your policy to help you with building the online e-commerce business you want to grow your wealth and bring financial security to you and your family.

6

-

Build a Permanent Line of Credit for Your Amazon Business

Mark Writes

One of the biggest reasons that business owners of any type go out of business is lack of capital.

That's why banks make so much money off small business owners.

They offer those juicy lines of credit that business owners desperately need, and in exchange for that access to the cash that business owners need, the bank take control of everything including the very cash they offered the business owner.

But what if it didn't need to be this way?

What if you could build a permanent line of credit for your Amazon e-commerce business? What if you knew that at any moment you had access to tens of thousands or even hundreds of thousands of dollars that could be a pool of money to purchase your inventory, or sit on inventory while you wait for it to sell? If you knew that your fourth-quarter was going to be a blowout season, you could use the line of credit to yourself to secure your business through the lean months in the springtime or summer when sales might be slower.

That's exactly what many of our clients who are engaged in e-commerce business do, with their Bank On Yourself policies.

Your e-commerce business needs cash to survive and thrive in a global Amazon marketplace. You have access to the cash value in your policy for any reason, at any time. Within about 3 to 5 business days, you can have those funds directly deposited into your business checking account to make inventory purchases or to float your business through a tough spot.

You also have no required repayment on the policies loan when you borrow against policy. This means you could technically go thirty days or ten years without repaying the policy loan, and as long as the policy remains in force, you could keep getting dividends and cash value growth even on the capital you borrowed.

Please understand however that you're shooting yourself in the foot if you never repay your policy loans.

The policy could lapse if the loan balance exceeds the cash value, and you could lose your death benefit. If there are gains, there would even be taxes due under that circumstance. Plus, when you pay back your loan to your policy, you free that money up to be spent again on something else (Q4 comes every year)!

So, be an honest banker with yourself and work with a competent advisor who can help you manage this asset for your convenience, and to help you repay your loans to your policy so you can use the cash for your next round of inventory, or your next car, and so on!

The Alternative

Let's take a moment to talk about the alternative.

The first option is that you save in a savings account to buy your inventory, and that you buy it hopefully at the right time when everything is on sale and then sell it on Amazon for a profit.

But how much interest was earning in your savings account while you waited? Virtually none with today's savings rates. And after you made the inventory purchases? None at all!

And what if it takes longer than expected to sell your inventory? What will you do if you don't have any cash available to run your business in the meantime?

Still, other people decide to use a credit card that offers a 60-day no payments option for their inventory, selling it before the 60 days are up. But what happens if it takes longer than 60 days to sell your inventory? Your interest rate on that credit card jumps up to 21%, and there go your profits. Not to mention your credit score.

By building a permanent line of credit to yourself inside a cash value life insurance policy (what we call Bank On Yourself), you become your own credit card, to yourself!

Danny Stock & Mark Willis

7

-

Use the Policy Loan Feature for Inventory (Repay on Your Terms)

Mark Writes

Not only does this strategy of becoming your own financing source give you more flexibility as a business owner, it gives you some growth on your money inside the policy at the same time.

An Example

Let's take a simple example and run that scenario out.

Let's say you need to buy some inventory for your Amazon business, and you don't have any capital saved in a Bank On Yourself policy or even any cash saved at the local bank.

What is your last option?

If you're going to buy the inventory to-day, you have to take a traditional bank financing loan at 10% for $10,000 to buy your inventory. Let's say that it takes you an entire year to repay that bank loan, meaning your inventory took twelve months to sell and get shipped out.

That would be a monthly payment of $879.16 over 12 months. The total payment would be $10,549.89. Do you know where you're going to come up with $879 a month? What if your inventory doesn't sell like you hope it will? Will the bank be forgiving? Or will they wreck your credit score and repossess your inventory? Will they jack up your interest rate if you miss a few payments? And for the privilege, you'll pay not only the $10,000 back, but an extra $549 comes out of your pocket as profits to the bank.

Most people can pretty quickly figure out that the bank is the one holding all the chips in this situation while you take all the risk. There's no risk for a bank. If you don't sell your inventory on time, the bank just collects your money another way either through higher interest rates or forcing you to sell other assets like your car or repossessing the inventory.

But what about paying cash for your Amazon inventory? Isn't that the best way to go?

Let's take that same example and walk it out using cash.

Let's say you've been able to sock away $10,000 into a regular bank savings account. First of all, good for you for being a diligent saver and living within your means. It also tells me that you are able to consistently sock money away somewhere and that's a good thing.

However, now you're faced with a dilemma.

If you withdraw the money out of your savings account, how much interest are you now earning on that money? Of course, you're earning nothing on money you take out of a bank account. The money is gone from your savings account and $0 is left in your savings to earn you interest.

This principle of "opportunity cost" is true whether you are pulling the money from a savings account, a CD, a brokerage account, a 401(k), or a hedge fund. There is no avoiding the problem of opportunity cost with traditional saving and investing vehicles.

The truth is that you finance everything you buy. Either you pay interest to a bank, or you pass up interest you could have earned on the money that you left invested instead.

The Net Zero Status

Most people are tied down to "net zero" and are either on the savers or debtor staircase.

Either you take a loan and fall below net zero where you're then forced to climb and scratch your way up the staircase back to the net zero line, only to fall back into debt again (More inventory is needed! A newer car! The kids need to go to college!). Or, you climb up the staircase of saving only to crash back down again when you withdraw the money from whatever account you were saving it in. You've lost not only what was in the savings account, but also whatever amount that money would have earned had you not spent the money!

Avoiding the Opportunity Cost

I said earlier there's no way to avoid the problem of opportunity cost with traditional saving and investing vehicles.

But what if you could overcome the problem with a Bank On Yourself type whole life policy? With a Bank On Yourself whole life policy designed with non-direct recognition loans, you're able to lift off from net zero, and build wealth the way banks do, letting your money work in two places at once!

When you borrow against your life insurance policy, if it's properly designed by a

Bank On Yourself Authorized Advisor who knew what he or she was doing, your money continues to build and grow even on the capital you borrowed.

Let's see it in action.

A Bank On Yourself Scenario

So, let's say that you have a Bank On Yourself policy with $10,000 in cash value and $200,000 in a death benefit. Let's say you'd like to purchase some inventory for your Amazon business.

You simply go on to your policy website, request a loan, and the funds arrive in your bank account in about three to five business days. You then simply pay cash for your inventory as usual. Meanwhile, the policy's still earning dividends and guaranteed annual cash value increases as if you never touched a dime of it! Then, let's say you repaid the loan on the policy over the course of the next 6 months.

Even though you have a loan against your policy, the insurance company doesn't care how or when or if you pay off the loan.

If you take the loan all the way to your grave, the death benefit is simply reduced by the remaining loan balance when you pass away. In other words, the loan is self-collateralized by the life insurance policy itself.

Genius!

This is the safest loan a life insurance company can offer, and it allows you the tremendous advantage of overcoming the problem of always being stuck on net zero.

Value and Interest

Now, please don't overlook the fact that there is loan interest that's applied on policy loans. Over the course of the year, simple interest accrues on policy loans, and you don't want to forget about that.

Calculated on a 6 month schedule at 5% simple interest compounded annually in arrears, your total interest capitalized would be $119.73. Now why would you willingly take a $10,000 loan and get charged $119.73? Aren't you paying interest on your own money?

Think about it. Where did that $119 end up? You guessed it, back in the insurance company that you essentially own (along with all the other policyholders)! What did your policy earn at the same time that you were charged loan interest? Most well-engineered policies over a long period of time can do something in the ballpark of 4 to 7% IRR. I've seen it lower and I've seen it higher but that range is pretty common. So, over the course of that year you got compound growth on 5.5% which turns out to be $550. Now you really did pay $119 of interest so you have to subtract that from the gains you made, but even so that's still a net-positive of $430.

Which would you rather have? $430? Or $0? *Is this better or worse than just paying cash for your inventory?*

If you used bank financing, you'd pay $549.00 in interest that you'll never see again.

An Amazon Inventory Review

If you use your policy, you get access to capital with no questions asked. And while you do pay interest on policy loans, that interest ultimately benefits you through a combination of guaranteed annual increases plus any dividends the company pays.

That means both the principal and interest you pay can ultimately end up in your policy for you to use again and again, to buy and sell more Amazon inventory (or for whatever you want).

The money you borrow is working for you in two ways simultaneously – growing your policy without skipping a beat... and generating profits for you in your Amazon business.

And it's not just a matter of numbers.

Again, what happens when you take a loan is that *you* control the repayment process from start to finish. If your inventory sells quickly, you can pay off the loan quickly and then pull the money out again for your next inventory purchasing cycle. If you have high-end products that take longer to sell, the policy is just content enough to sit on the sidelines until everything is off the Amazon shelves.

By using this loan feature, you're able to establish yourself as the most competitive in the Amazon Marketplace. You immediately move yourself to the front of the line and can more effectively price your products, selling them at higher margins. No longer are you under the gun to sell your inventory to pay off a debt.

You could even use your credit card to get the free airline miles or free t-shirt or whatever, then pay off the credit card 3 to 5 days later from your policy loan. Just be sure you have it in your policy before you swipe that credit card!

8

-

Bank On Yourself is a Warehouse of Wealth for Your Amazon Profits!

Mark Writes

So now, we are lifting off from net zero. You've hit that escape velocity, and you're really beginning to build profits in your Amazon business because you're not having a to deal with traditional banks.

Your Money Will Work for You

What will you do with all the profit that you're generating from your Amazon business? Maybe it will give you the chance to quit your day job. Maybe it's a chance for you to bring your spouse home from work or to enjoy the lifestyle that you truly want. But where will all that money go? All the money that you don't spend is known as "discretionary income." And your money has to live someplace. If you think about it, where your money lives will make it do different things.

Take for example a certificate of deposit at a local bank. A lot of people think that CDs are a good place to stash cash. I'm not so sure. These days CDs aren't paying much interest. CDs wrap your money up and you can't access your funds without penalizing you. In addition, the growth is taxable while you wait.

Not *my* idea of a great bargain!

Now there are hundreds of places you can put your money and we've been talking about one of them in great detail. Dividend-paying whole life insurance designed for maximum cash accumulation: what we call *Bank On Yourself* policies. In my opinion, there's no better place for your money to reside.

We've already talked about how you can access the money for your Amazon business, but what about all the other things you might need the money for? Cars, vacations, home repairs, medical emergencies, your kids' college, and ultimately retirement income all of which require monies that have to live somewhere.

The Future of Your Money

If all your money is spread around twelve different financial vehicles (checking, savings, 401(k), credit cards, home equity, 529 plans... the list goes on), what kind of a dent can you make on all these massive expenses that your life requires?

It's like if I had a hundred pebbles in my hand and if I threw them as hard as I could at a window – they would not shatter the window. However, when I drop all the pebbles and pick up a big rock, breaking the window is no problem at all.

It's all about focus.

We've talked a lot about how this can be put to use in your Amazon business, but I want you to take a moment to think about its other applications.

Does having your money safe and available for whatever you need take away any of your options?

Let's say your kids need to go to college. Did you know that having your money in life insurance keeps it off the radar of the FAFSA and CSS profiles? That means more financial aid may be available for your student, and less money may be expected from your family.

Let's say that you need to pay your property tax every year. You can either leave that money in your escrow account with the bank, or you could just simply pull it from your Bank On Yourself policy every year, when the tax is due, and then repay the policy loan on the life insurance all year long, all the while getting cash value increases and dividends on the money you used to pay your taxes.

I could go on and on. There are infinite applications of the self-financing function in your life.

That said, saving up for the day when your earned income stops is still an essential part of responsible retirement planning. Income will stop, but expenses never stop for as long as you live. So how can Bank On yourself help you with that problem?

There are several tax advantages afforded to life insurance in the tax code. Life insurance even predates the income tax system in this country! By taking a combination of return of basis withdrawals and tax-free loans, you can access the entire cash value both principal and gains tax free.

> **Note:** This of course is under current tax law, so keep voting.

It's also important to understand that if you take out huge loans that you never repay, and then lapse your policy, or over withdraw beyond your cost basis, gains are taxable outside of your life insurance policy. This is just another reason why you should be working with a competent Bank On Yourself Authorized Advisor who can keep you from running into such pitfalls.

In our most recent tax reform in 2017, through all the tax changes that were made to the individual tax code, the tax treatment of life insurance was essentially left untouched. That should tell you something about how Congress views this asset! In fact, many congressmen and women have life insurance in their portfolios. (Now you know the real reason why they didn't bother this asset.)

I know many people, in fact many of my clients, who are enjoying six-figure income on their life insurance policies and reporting $0 on their income taxes.

Remember, your money has to live somewhere. Where do you want it to live? Is it doing what you want it to do? Or, like a handful of pebbles, is it spread around so much that it's not doing anything at all very well?

Let Bank On Yourself be a warehouse of wealth for your Amazon profits.

Danny Stock & Mark Willis

9

-

Use Bank On Yourself to Pay off Your Debts to Amazon Lending and to Other Creditors

Mark Writes

What if you're in debt? Should you pay down your debt before starting Bank On Yourself?

Paying off credit cards and loans makes sound financial sense, of course, and that's why some people try to pay off as much as they can each month. That often leaves little left at the end of the month for savings.

One client recently was paying $600 to $800 a month more than the minimum payment due on his credit cards, in an attempt to eliminate his debt as quickly as possible. We ran an analysis and discovered that if he paid just the minimum balance due each month, and put the difference into a Bank On Yourself policy where it would grow for him safely and predictably, he could potentially have an additional $50,000 at retirement!

With the debts you've already got - what would it look like to recoup the interest currently leaving your pocket and actually start earning that interest yourself?

Are you in debt? You could start now and reduce or eliminate debt while at the same time increasing savings. Our clients realize that with Bank On Yourself, they can help their families move from being debtors, to savers, to wealth accumulators!

Using Your Debt

Here's how it works: Imagine a huge pile of cash - your debt. Now imagine it's slowly coming down as you make at least the minimum payments on that debt.

Next to that pile of debt, imagine your Bank On Yourself policy and start packing as much as you can into your own "bank." Now, imagine that money which starts small begins to grow *very* quickly. At some point in the future, those two amounts of cash equal each other (the amount you *owe*, and what you *own* in your policy).

Simply take a loan from your policy and wipe out all your debt. Now you're debt-free to everyone except your own "bank."

Meanwhile, you keep earning interest and dividends on the full value in the policy!

Sorry Dave Ramsey, but this is better than "debt-free"!

Being Your Own Banker Gives You Options!

Meanwhile, now that you're your own banker, you can adjust payments to your policy loan, reduce, increase, skip… it's all under your control.

If you had a job loss or income emergency, and you still had your debts with *other* people's banks... would they give you a break? No! They'd kick you while you were down. They'd wreck your credit score. They'd raise your interest rate. They'd repo your car. But at *your* "bank," you're able to have peace of mind to lower or stop repayments.

Should I wait till I'm debt free to start a Bank on Yourself policy?

Most of the time, *No!*

We had a client who had $18,123 in credit card debt, averaging 9.53% She was using the "snowball method." She was overpaying but a few hundred dollars on her policy and wanted to know if paying that off first would make more sense than doing the "snowball method" and she brought us a spreadsheet showing it would take her 36 months to pay off the credit cards. She was curious if it made more sense to pay down the debt before starting Bank On Yourself.

We told her, that Bank On Yourself is Dave Ramsey's Snowball Method on steroids. This is the Snow*BANK* Method!

We taught her that, rather than just throwing extra cash at the credit cards, that by paying the minimums on her cards and shoveling everything on top of that to her own bank - her life insurance policy would work out in the long run for her. Using her cash value to "buy back her debt" one credit card at a time, she was able to continue getting growth on the cash she used in the policy to pay off the credit cards.

What was the true cost of her credit cards?

She owed $18,123. But the true cost was also the three *years* (time) it took to pay them off - and the lost savings she could have been earning in her policy. If she started her policy now to help pay off the credit cards, by age 70 she could have $479,547 versus having only $411,207 if she waited just three years to get started.

Those credit cards cost her not just $18,123, but also a missed retirement income of $68,340! That means her total cost of her credit cards was $86,463 (18K + 68K)!

Dave Ramsey and Suze Orman would tell us to pay down debt before starting to save… we (and the *math*!) disagree wholeheartedly…

Conclusion

Danny Concludes

By this point, I am sure you have realized the potential that firing your banker and becoming your own banker grants you!

I cannot tell you how often I have made financial mistakes in my life that cost me untold amounts of money in retirement. My solemn wish is that you use what is learned here and take action!

Oftentimes, we sit on information or knowledge and never implement what is taught. This is one time that you should not hesitate to move forward. The longer you wait, the longer you will continue to do what all of the general population has been told to do and be stuck in a continual cycle of debt, interest payments, and your money managing you.

I have always taught in my Amazon groups that if everyone else is doing something, then maybe you should do it differently. This is how I have always viewed selling on Amazon; I chose to view my finances and investments in the same manner.

Living my life this way and going against the grain as they say has given me a life of freedom and prosperity that will last my family for generations.

My passion has always been to help others and serve those who wish to discover the true freedom that exists just on the other side. If you find yourself stuck in the day to day with seemingly no end in sight to your struggles and work, then take a moment to look underneath the surface of the "information" that exists about making money and investing it.

You're off to a life-altering start if you have made it this far. Take one more step and join me on the other side.

Here's to your financial future being prosperous!

~ Danny Stock
www.amzlegends.com

Mark Concludes

So how do you actually take action after reading something like this? You may be left with questions and ideas that this short book could not cover. You may want to see some of this with your own numbers in mind.

While I think everyone should know about this strategy and the benefits that it offers, there is certainly cost to be considered as well. For example, even with the more modern whole life policy designs, there are still a few years in the early part of the policy that you are overcoming the initial cost of insurance.

For those who need a hundred percent of their money right now and have no interest in future growth, I recommend a shoebox or a savings account. If you need 30% rate of return every year, you might look elsewhere. But for those that can live within their means and can learn to think like a banker, this strategy holds tremendous power and freedom.

So, what do you do?

I recommend a competent financial professional who has been trained and authorized by Bank On Yourself to look over your specific situation and see if Bank On Yourself would be a good fit for you.

Unfortunately, there are a lot of advisors out there who have stumbled across this concept and have said, "Oh yeah, I can do that." I'll sometimes see their clients are bringing this book or *The Bank On Yourself Revolution* book to their CPA or investment advisor and they will do a quick skim of it, and then dismiss it without really understanding it. I've even seen many insurance agents Google the term during a meeting with a client and say they can set this up.

Not so!

If you work with the wrong insurance company, or if the agent who designed it for you didn't build your policy correctly, your policy could grow too slowly, you could lose some of the tax benefits, or both. Your policy might also have a disastrous loan provision which penalizes you when you access your money. What you don't know (or your advisor doesn't know) *can* hurt you.

That may be why the Bank On Yourself Authorized Advisor program was created. The Bank On Yourself Authorized Advisor can fix the problems sometimes associated with a "me-too advisor," and may also help bring some clarity to the process of becoming your own source of financing using the strategy of Bank On Yourself.

The words Bank On Yourself® have a specific meaning and have even been trademarked. When you work with a Bank On Yourself Authorized Advisor, you know with confidence you are working with someone who understands all these intricacies and can build the policy correctly for you and your business.

My team of associates and I have been Bank On Yourself Authorized Advisors for many years. Next to my CFP® designation, mastering the Bank On Yourself strategy is the most advanced and nuanced training I have ever been through as a financial professional.

It's truly an honor to be a part of this elite group of only about 200 advisors around the country! Even more, it is an honor to see the lives of our clients changing and becoming financially free.

If you would like to have a free no-obligation financial consultation to hear a bit more about how this might look in your circumstance, schedule an appointment with us. We don't charge a fee to have a simple 15-minute phone call with you. And we work all over the United States. We work with Authorized Advisors in Canada as well.

Simply head to:

www.lakegrowth.com/schedule

and schedule your free 15-minute phone appointment. This gives you a no-pressure chance to meet and ask any question that this report didn't answer, get to know me or someone on my team, and we can schedule a follow-up meeting to have a more in-depth conversation with you. Make sure to mention Danny or "Amazon Legends book" in the notes so we know how you heard about this!

www.lakegrowth.com/schedule

(Choose "phone introduction.")

My hope is that you will take this and act before the end of the day on what you've learned here. Studies show that if you go past 24 hours and don't do something about a new piece of information, you lose it. Heck, sometimes I can walk into another room and forget why I walked in there!

So, take two minutes now while it's fresh on your mind and schedule that appointment; you have a lifetime of financial wealth to gain.

You chose wisely to team up with the Amazon Legends. I hope I can be a resource to your journey and building a successful business and the life you love.

All the best!

Mark Willis
www.lakegrowth.com/schedule

Disclaimers

Important Notice

While a great deal of care has been taken to provide accurate and current information regarding the subject matter covered, neither Danny Stock, Amazon Legends, Mark Willis, Lake Growth, Inc., Bank On Yourself®, or Pamela Yellen are responsible for any errors or omissions, or for the results obtained from the use of this information. The ideas, suggestions, general principles and conclusions presented here are subject to local, state and federal laws and regulations and revisions of same, and are intended for informational purposes only. All information in this Report is provided "as is," with no guarantee of completeness, accuracy, or timeliness regarding the results obtained from the use of this information. And without warranty of any kind, express or implied, including but not limited to warranties of performance, merchantability, and fitness for a particular purpose.

Your use of this information is at your own risk. You assume full responsibility and risk of loss resulting from the use of this information.

Danny Stock, Amazon Legends, Mark Willis, Lake Growth, Inc., Bank On Yourself®, or Pamela Yellen will not be held liable for any direct, special, indirect, incidental, consequential, or punitive damages or any other damages whatsoever, whether in an action based upon a statute, contract, tort (including, but not limited to negligence), or otherwise, relating to the use of this information.

Neither Danny Stock, Amazon Legends, Mark Willis, Lake Growth, Inc., Bank On Yourself®, or Pamela Yellen are engaged in rendering legal, accounting, or other professional services. If accounting, financial, legal, or tax advice is required, the services of a competent professional should be sought.